Real Life Habits for ˆ

SO-DRE-679

world vision
p u b l i s h i n g

Written & Compiled by:
Jeffrey Lawrence Benjamin
Michael B. Kitson
John Oliver
Thomas J. Powell

i

Book design by: Mike Kitson
Cover Design by: Alex Leutzinger, Annaliese Miller & Gib Leiker
Cover Photo by: John Thomas Ravizé

World Vision Publishing, LLC
COPYRIGHT © 2003, World Vision Publishing, LLC
All rights reserved
Printed in the United States of America
03 02 01 00 99 12 11 10 9 8 7 6

Library of Congress Catalog Card Number: 200312301
ISBN 0-9727173-0-7

world vision
p u b l i s h i n g

Also by these authors:

Real Life Habits for Success – Achieve Your Goals
Real Life Habits for Success – Master Your Communication
Real Life Habits for Success – Maximize Your Time

Special Thanks:

Cindie Geddes

Dedication:

This book is dedicated to those people
who want to improve the quality of their lives.

FOREWORD

All it takes is one great idea, one little sentence, a simple concept, reinforced by action to bring an abundance of prosperity and success into your life. This is the central idea of this book.

We are living in a moment in time that humanity has dreamed about for millenniums. However, with all the modern conveniences and technical miracles there comes a price. To enjoy our lives fully and truly be without the debilitating affects of stress, we need the tools and habits to help put it all in perspective.

Stress is any action or situation that places physical or psychological demand on you. Anything that tends to throw you off balance can be a stressor. A divorce is stressful but so is marriage. Positive and negative events both require adjustment and adaptation.

Study after study has shown life events of all types (buying or selling a house, losing a job, being promoted, moving to a new location, surgery, etc.) are significant stressors that can lead to physical and psychological problems. Two-thirds of visits to family physicians are for stress-related symptoms, and three-fourths of modern disease is related to stress.

Some degrees of stress are important for human development. Stress can help us grow in every area of life, much like the body and mind of an athlete are stretched to new incredible levels by inducing stress through vigorous exercises. Stress can help you perform your best. Too little or too much stress can produce poor results. The key is to notice when you are in a state of stress, then transform it to work in your favor.

Packed within these pages are simple and practical suggestions to help you improve your life. Invest a little time in reading this book, experiment with some of our suggestions and then watch as a world of opportunity opens up before you. You will find that your work, your

relationships and your sanity are all improved just by incorporating a few small changes into your thoughts and actions.

Best of success to you!

"A man is not hurt so much by what happens as by his opinion of what happens."

Michel Montainge

HABIT ~ 1

DISTINGUISH WHAT IS TRIVIAL AND WHAT IS IMPORTANT

To lead a tranquil life, learn to differentiate between what is trivial and what is important. The way you perceive and react to situations determines whether you'll be stressed or relaxed. Use this question to get a handle on the difference: "Is this going to matter 10 years from now?"

"I am only one, but still I am one. I cannot do everything, but I can do something. I will not refuse to do the something I can do."

Helen Keller

HABIT ~ 2

ENJOY THE RELAXING PHYSICAL SENSATION OF BREATHING PEACEFULLY

Whenever you feel anxious or nervous, take a few deep breaths, inhaling through the nose and exhaling through the mouth. When breathing out, say to yourself, "three." On the next out-breath, "two." Continue to "one" and repeat the cycle. This will send a message to your brain and body that it's time to relax and calm down.

"We cannot hold a torch to light another's path without brightening our own."

Ben Sweetland

HABIT ~ 3

USE CANDLES AND AROMATIC SCENTS AT HOME AND/OR WORK

The calming effects of candles and aromatherapy can help put you at ease. Experiment with different scents. Place the candles at a variety of levels. Allow yourself to float with the experience.

"The weak can never forgive.
Forgiveness is the attribute
of the strong."

Mohandas Gandhi

HABIT ~ 4

PRACTICE THE ART OF FORGIVENESS

The person who seeks revenge should dig two graves. The act of forgiveness is actually an act of self-care as it releases anger, resentment, pain or fear, and allows room for joy, happiness, peace and love. Forgiveness is something you do for yourself, not for others. You can achieve forgiveness by writing a letter to a person who has offended you. Say everything you want to say and then destroy the letter. Another tool that may help is to talk to the person if possible, owning the part of the issue that is yours. Or speak with a trusted friend, clergy or counselor to get constructive feedback.

"Each morning when I open my eyes I say to myself: "I, not events, have the power to make me happy or unhappy today. I can choose which it will be. Yesterday is dead, tomorrow hasn't arrived yet. I have just one day, today, and I'm going to be happy in it."

Groucho Marx

HABIT ~ 5

USE AUTO-SUGGESTION

An easy and effective technique for body relaxation involves auto-suggestion. Doctors and psychologists have been using this internal verbal instruction technique for centuries. You simply give yourself a command such as: "I am relaxed and at ease," or "I am calm and relaxed." Repeat the command until your body accepts it.

"True enjoyment comes from
activity of the mind and
exercise of the body;
the two are united."

Alexander von Humboldt

HABIT ~ 6

MAINTAIN A REGULAR EXERCISE PROGRAM

Numerous studies conclude that exercise results in measurable improvements in relieving depression and anxiety due to stress. Studies show physical activity is positively associated with good mental health, especially positive mood, general well being and less stress overall. Exercising three to five times a week can serve as a buffer for stress. Try jogging, walking, racquetball, basketball, swimming, aerobics, dancing, weight training—whatever works for you.

"The greatest discovery of any generation is that human beings can alter their lives by altering the attitudes of their minds."

Albert Schweitzer

HABIT ~ 7

BUILD AND SIT BY A FIRE

The ritual of gathering wood alone can help relax you. Lose your thoughts in the flames as you watch them dance across the logs. Feel the heat on your face as you forget time and space and transcend to a state of peacefulness.

"There is in the worst fortunes
the best of chances for
a happy change."

Euripides

HABIT ~ 8

PUT YOURSELF IN TIME OUT

As you become aware of your suffering mood or inappropriate behavior, take a break. Relieve yourself and others around you by excusing yourself and demagnifying the moment. Counting to 100 may help.

"Action may not always
bring happiness, but
there is no happiness
without action."

Benjamin Disraeli

HABIT ~ 9

PREPARE FOR TOMORROW
BEFORE YOU GO TO SLEEP EACH NIGHT

Before going to bed get your clothes out and ready for the next day. If you need to make lunches or pack the work you brought home, do it before you retire each night. The benefit of this is you don't have to feel rushed in the morning, running around like a lunatic.

"Acceptance of what has happened is the first step to overcoming the consequences of any misfortune."

William James

HABIT ~ 10

TAKE CHANGE BY THE HAND
BEFORE IT TAKES YOU BY THE THROAT

For thousands of years, sages and philosophers have said in one way or another: "The only constant force in the world is change." Today, however, change is moving at such a rapid pace that most people are unable to cope with it effectively. Entire industries are forced to adapt to change or suffer the consequences—extinction! To be able to survive requires us to view change as a positive force offering hidden treasures to be uncovered and found. Embrace change!

"The secret of getting ahead is getting started. The secret of getting started is breaking your complex, overwhelming tasks into small, manageable tasks, and then starting the first one."

Mark Twain

HABIT ~ 11

BREAK GOALS DOWN INTO SMALLER GOALS

How do you eat a dinosaur? One bite at a time! Breaking goals down into smaller, more manageable goals helps dismantle feelings of being overwhelmed. It also provides a system for achieving a series of smaller goals that build feelings of success and achievement. As each small goal is achieved, your skill level and confidence will rise, eventually enabling you to accomplish any goal you desire.

"All work is as seed sown: it grows and spreads and sows itself anew."

Thomas Carlyle

HABIT ~ 12

USE A ONE MINUTE
BODY RELAXATION TECHNIQUE

Body relaxation is the first step in learning how to eliminate tension. Remove extraneous stimuli and allow yourself to be alert and to concentrate more intensely while being relaxed at the same time. The technique can be performed lying down or sitting in a chair. Close your eyes. Starting from the head, slowly scan your body all the way to your toes. As you scan, notice any tension in the body (on the forehead, around the eyes, clenched hand, etc.), then relax the area by saying the word "relax."

"In most cases, it takes only a few minor adjustments to dramatically improve performance."

Jeffrey Lawrence Benjamin

HABIT ~ 13

WORK HARDER ON YOURSELF
THAN YOU DO ON YOUR JOB

Make *kaizen*, (the Japanese word for constant and never-ending improvement) one of your mantras. Each day look for one activity in your life that you can do just a little bit better. Whether it is five more sit-ups, three new vocabulary words, or better eating habits, each small accomplishment builds increased self-confidence.

"In any moment of decision the best thing you can do is the right thing, the next best thing is the wrong thing, and the worst thing you can do is nothing."

Theodore Roosevelt

HABIT ~ 14

USE YOUR LAYOVER AT THE AIRPORT

Have you ever felt as though you were imprisoned in an airport? The key is to plan ahead. Take a book along to read or write a letter to someone special. Nowadays airports are starting to add fitness centers as well. The important thing is to plan to do something you enjoy so you don't fall prey to the stress and anxiety often found in airports.

"The business of life is not business, but living."

B.C. Forbes

HABIT ~ 15

ESTABLISH A REGULAR SLEEPING SCHEDULE

A sound sleep can restore you both mentally and physically. Yet according to national surveys, between 15 and 20 percent of the adult population routinely suffers from insomnia. Chronic insomnia is often triggered by anxiety, but it may persist even after the source of stress is removed. If you cannot fall asleep in 15 to 20 minutes, read until you feel drowsy. No matter when you fall asleep, always get up at the same time.

"In three words I can sum up everything I've learned about life. 'It goes on.'"

Robert Frost

HABIT ~ 16

LEARN TO LET GO

We all have had experiences in life that we have rewound and reviewed dozens of times in our minds. When we tune into ourselves and listen to our own self-talk we hear some thoughts and feelings that we want to release from our minds. If you are able to turn off your mind-chatter at night and fall comfortably asleep, you are already practicing letting go. People who have insomnia often have difficulty letting go of the day's details or upcoming events. If you are one of these unlucky souls, try writing out everything that is on your mind. Get it out of your head and onto the page. The key is to recognize the thought or feeling and consciously let go of it.

"You gain strength, courage, and confidence by every experience in which you look fear in the face. You must do the thing you think you cannot do."

Eleanor Roosevelt

HABIT ~ 17

FEEL THE FEAR AND GO FOR IT

How many times have you scared yourself out of doing something? The concern, worry or terror continued to grow bigger until you were immobilized by the fear. When you really want to do something and it is the fear that is holding you back, then acknowledge that you are fearful and do it anyway. The only way to conquer fear is to push through it by taking immediate action.

"I look back on my life like a
good day's work, it was done
and I feel satisfied with it."

Grandma Moses

HABIT ~ 18

BE RESPONSIBLE TO YOURSELF FOR YOUR HAPPINESS

Empower yourself to be responsible for your own happiness. It is not the government's responsibility to make you happy; it is not up to your parents, your significant other, your friends, your boss, society, or even God. Look for the joy in everything you do and enjoy the day on purpose and by choice.

"Without struggle there
is no progress."

Fredrick Douglas

HABIT ~ 19

NURTURE THE BELIEF THAT EVERY CRISIS IS A LEARNING OPPORTUNITY

If you were to recall an experience you had in the past that was at the time a "crisis," it is quite possible, in hindsight, that it was one of the best and most rewarding learning experiences you've had. Look for the lesson in all challenges.

"While we may not be able to control all that happens to us, we can control what happens inside us."

Ben Franklin

HABIT ~ 20

TAKE A MUSICAL SOUND BATH

This exercise helps you clear away noise and sounds that have bombarded you during your day. Select a tape or disc of your favorite relaxation music. Lie down or sit in a comfortable position and turn on the music. Take several deep breaths and let go of all tension. Allow the music to flow through you and over you, washing away all the junk noise and sounds that have pounded you all day. Let yourself get immersed in the music.

"Life is a mirror and will
reflect back to the thinker
what he thinks into it."

Ernest Homes

HABIT ~ 21

PLAY MORE OFTEN

Playing keeps you laughing and smiling. Even the thought of being playful helps you be lighthearted and relaxed. Have you come across people who have lost their sense of playfulness? Stress is all over their faces, and no one wants to be around them. If you want to enhance your life experience, enjoy some of these stress reducing playful activities: You can tickle someone, roll around on the floor, smile, run, call a childhood friend, keep a great attitude for an entire day, or do any activity that you consider playful. Feel how you are becoming more easygoing, happy and relaxed.

"Let freedom reign. The sun never set on so glorious a human achievement."

Nelson Mandela

HABIT ~ 22

DO THINGS JUST FOR THE FUN OF IT

Forget about being an adult. Be a kid again, fascinated and excited with the simple things in life. Whether it is skipping down the hall at the office or building a snowman, we can all benefit by not taking life too seriously and building more playful fun time into life.

"If you would not be forgotten
as soon as you are gone,
either write things worth
reading or do things
worth writing about."

Benjamin Franklin

HABIT ~ 23

PURCHASE A DIARY TO RECORD YOUR THOUGHTS AND FEELINGS

Experts and non-experts alike agree that writing your thoughts and feelings out on paper for a few minutes each day can help you feel renewed and ready to overcome any new challenges. It also provides you with a chance to script out successful and triumphant moments that you can call upon for strength.

"Always think of what
you have to do as easy
and it will be so."

Emile Coue

HABIT ~ 24

PRACTICE PROGRESSIVE RELAXATION

In order to relax it is important to know how tension and relaxation feel. Dr. Emund Jacobson, an American physician, conducted research on muscle physiology with an emphasis on relaxation. Jacobson proved that people can become aware of tension and learn how to relax. In progressive relaxation, Jacobson has people work on different areas of the body, one by one, contracting muscles, then letting go, and then finally allowing the whole body to relax.

"We ourselves feel that what we are doing is just a drop in the ocean. But the ocean would be less because of that missing drop."

Mother Teresa

HABIT ~ 25

AN HOUR BEFORE BEDTIME, TAKE A WARM BATH OR SHOWER

Gently rub sea salt over your feet, knees, thighs, shoulders, torso and arms. The warm water softens the skin, making it easy for the sea salt to draw out toxins, and the massage relieves muscle cramps and tension.

"Success is more a function
of consistent common sense
than it is of genius."

Ann Wang

HABIT ~ 26

AVOID ARTIFICIAL STIMULATING SUBSTANCES

Avoid drinking coffee, tea, colas or any other beverage containing caffeine within four hours of bedtime. Avoid alcohol and other drugs that will disrupt your sleep. Don't smoke before going to bed: Nicotine can be stimulating. Rest, refill, rejuvenate.

"The important medicine is tender love and care."

Mother Teresa

HABIT ~ 27

SLEEP ON A COMFORTABLE BED

People are known to sleep on the same bed for ten, twenty, or more years. The average person perspires eight ounces during each eight hours of sleep, and rolls over 50 to 80 times during the same period. Sleep on a good mattress that wicks away the sweat and supports you ergonomically. Be as picky as the Princess and the Pea and revel in the rewards of a good night's sleep.

"The greatest gift you can give others is to allow them to be themselves."

Bill Ussery

HABIT ~ 28

CONNECT WITH OTHERS

Connecting with others, networking and creating fulfilling relationships that are a positive influence in your life can be your single most important life purpose. Focus on others, be genuine and listen at least as much as you speak. Discover the goals, dreams and hopes of others. Having common goals, values and shared experiences enhances any relationship.

"It is our attitude
at the beginning of a
difficult undertaking which,
more than anything else,
will determine its outcome."

William James

HABIT ~ 29

RESPOND POSITIVELY INSTEAD OF REACTING NEGATIVELY

Inevitably you will encounter a situation when someone decides to "get in your face." This person can come in the form of an angry customer, an irate driver, an inconsiderate coworker or disgruntled boss. The key is to not let the other person throw you out of whack, to push you into the stress zone. Take a second to think before you respond, then do so in a positive fashion.

"Change is inevitable,
growth is optional."

Anonymous

HABIT ~ 30

ACCEPT WHAT YOU CANNOT CHANGE

Many people needlessly worry about things over which they have no control. The Serenity Prayer is a great reminder. We all know how it goes: God grant me the serenity to accept the things I cannot change and have the courage to change the things I can, and the wisdom to know the difference. It is easy to dismiss such familiar platitudes. Read the words again today and take them to heart.

"Real generosity toward the future consists in giving all to what is present."

Albert Camus

HABIT ~ 31

LIVE IN THE NOW

When you feel yourself stressing over anything, ask: "Where am I and what is the time?" As no one is capable of explaining exactly where we are in the universe, and time is only relative, the only truthful answer is HERE and NOW. Release yourself from thoughts of your past and future. Focus on this moment. Enjoy the peace that comes from living in the now!

"The only real security that a
person can have in the world
is a reserve of knowledge,
experience, and ability."

Henry Ford

HABIT ~ 32

EXPERIENCE THE LIBRARY

The library presents the opportunity to find knowledge and be imaginative. You can research or experience an infinite number of mental states or destinations. You create your destiny. Let your mind play with options for that destiny.

"Ten minutes of genuine belly laughter had an anesthetic effect and would give me at least two hours of pain-free sleep."

Norman Cousins

HABIT ~ 33

LAUGH AND HAVE FUN MORE OFTEN

Half of all Americans are experiencing toxic levels of stress in their hectic and challenging lives. Have fun, play and laugh out loud. One hundred laughs can increase the body's endorphins equivalent to ten minutes on a rowing machine. Finding the humor in a situation can be powerful medicine by stimulating the immune system, producing the natural pain killer endorphins, renewing spiritual energy and promoting personal resilience.

"He who cannot change
the very fabric of his thought
will never be able to
change reality, and will
never, therefore,
make any progress."

Anwar Sadat

HABIT ~ 34

REPLACE NEGATIVE SELF-TALK WITH POSITIVE SELF-TALK

Communication research demonstrates the average person communicates or carries on an internal dialogue at the rate of 500 to 600 words per minute. Some studies also indicate that 80 percent is negative or pessimistic in nature. We must learn to identify, challenge, remove and replace negative messages. A fantastic way to do this is to replace negative messages with positive ones. For example, when you hear yourself saying, "I'll goof up this speech because I'm so nervous," instead say, "I'll be able to do this. I may be a little nervous but I'll do just fine." Never underestimate the power of positive thinking.

"The difference between ordinary and extraordinary is that little extra."

Author Unknown

HABIT ~ 35

LISTEN TO RELAXATION TAPES

Whether it's a soothing voice or the sound of a mountain stream, relaxation tapes can calm the wildest beast within you. Find a quiet spot and let the sounds soothe your soul.

"The last of the
human freedoms—to
choose one's attitude in
any given set of circumstances,
to choose one's own way."

Viktor Frankl

HABIT ~ 36

CHOOSE YOUR THOUGHTS

Choose to think only of what you want, rather than what you don't want. You will bring into your life that which you think about. Consciously eliminate negative thoughts and concerns. Choose your thoughts; control your life.

"We have it in our power to
begin the world again."

Thomas Paine

HABIT ~ 37

USE BREATHING FOR MIND POWER

This strategy is versatile and portable, so it can go anywhere. It's invisible, so it can go right into an exam room, business meeting or, in fact, any location. It's fast and easy to do at any time, and it brings results within minutes. It's rhythmic breathing. Basic breathing exercises can be done regularly and are helpful if done immediately before any situation where you face a challenge, such as a critical meeting, exam or speech. Inhale through the nose for four beats. Slowly exhale through the mouth for another four beats. Repeat four times.

"Things should be
made as simple as possible,
but not any simpler."

Albert Einstein

HABIT ~ 38

KEEP IT SUPER SIMPLE

Give life a KISS! Look for and find the simplicity in your life challenges and events. Take the time to make a plan, before embarking on potentially complicated problems or situations. Solve your concerns on paper and enjoy the peace of mind.

"There is more to life than increasing its speed."

Mohandas Gandhi

HABIT ~ 39

GO FISHING

It's hard not to be relaxed and feel peaceful while fishing. Listen to the water or any part of nature. Be soothed by the mellow peace of the sport. Only keep what you can eat or release what you catch!

"Success is neither magical
nor mysterious. Success is
the natural consequence of
consistently applying
basic fundamentals."

Jim Rohn

HABIT ~ 40

BALANCE YOUR CHECKBOOK AND DRAFT A BUDGET

Anxiety levels tend to rise when financial pressures such as monthly bills and unexpected expenses pop up. You're not alone if this happens to you. Surveys suggest that nearly 80 percent of those polled worry to some extent about paying their bills and making ends meet. You can combat this and win the battle by accounting for the money you spend and developing a budget that accommodates your personal financial parameters.

"The way people move is their autobiography in motion."

Gerry Spence

HABIT ~ 41

ENERGIZE YOUR BODY AND SOUL WITH POWER YOGA

Power yoga gives you a high-energy workout that builds strength, increases flexibility and develops concentration. You can rent an instructional video tape or take a class. One of the benefits of yoga is that you don't need any machines or weights to get a great workout. You can enjoy it without leaving your home or hotel room.

"Great things are done
by a series of small things
brought together."

Vincent van Gogh

HABIT ~ 42

STAY ORGANIZED

When you come upon a disorganized situation take the time to recognize your own discomforting symptoms. Recent studies have proven that organized individuals have lower blood pressure and live in a substantially more relaxed state of mind than those living and working in cluttered environments. Not only are organized people more relaxed, they get more done in less time!

"The reward of a thing well done is to have done it."

Ralph Waldo Emerson

HABIT ~ 43

FOCUS ON ONE THING AT A TIME

Make your desk completely empty except for the one item you're working with—nothing else, not even a pencil sharpener. Let nothing divert your attention from the task at hand. Do this and you'll be surprised at the clarity you will gain. Your creativity will increase, and your entire body will assume a disposition you'll thrive on.

"Opportunities are limited
only by our imagination."

Jonathan Sneen

HABIT ~ 44

PUT A FISH AQUARIUM IN YOUR OFFICE

An aquarium can calm you down. In a study of stress in dental patients, researchers found that patients who had a fish tank to look at in the waiting room showed lower anxiety levels than those who had none. Contemplating fish was even more effective than hypnosis in allaying patients' fears.

"When you get to the end of
your rope, tie a knot and
hang on. And swing!"

Leo Buscalia

HABIT ~ 45

MAKE A LIST OF THINGS YOU ENJOY DOING

Doing what you enjoy focuses your mind on the positive aspects of life. When you are doing what you enjoy you have more commitment and energy. Have fun with your favorite hobby. Run, play, read, write, listen, watch, ride, sail, drive or just imagine yourself enjoying whatever it is you have fun doing.

"Our life is what our thoughts make it."

Marcus Aurelius

HABIT ~ 46

DRAW A LINE BETWEEN WORK AND HOME

Draw a line between your work life and your other important life experiences. No one is exempt from the stress created when office work is brought home. It's fine to work at home; however, having a separate room, phone lines and environment helps you delineate "home" from "work." Know when to shut off work and give your attention to other areas of life such as family, recreation, health and fitness. Too much work without balance in other areas of life creates guilt and resentment, which in turn creates stress.

"The secret of genius is to carry the spirit of the child into old age, which means never losing your enthusiasm."

Aldous Huxley

HABIT ~ 47

ABANDON THE BELIEF
THAT YOU'RE TOO OLD

Sadly, an incredible amount of the population suffers from limiting beliefs about what they are capable of when they reach an age they consider old. Determine what you define as old and challenge such labels. Determine what you define as exciting and fun, then do more of it.

"There is nothing so useless as doing efficiently that which should not be done at all."

Peter F. Drucker

HABIT ~ 48

LEARN TO SAY NO
WITHOUT FEELING GUILTY

Saying no to another volunteer activity, a special assignment at work or even a social engagement can give you more free time or more time to attend to other commitments. Remember, saying no gets easier the more often you assert yourself. Say no with confidence, without feeling guilty!

"The palest ink is
more powerful than
the best memory."

Chinese Proverb

HABIT ~ 49

USE A PHONE AND ADDRESS DATA BOOK

Have you ever driven yourself crazy searching for an address or phone number that you needed? It's a great idea to have a central place for keeping this vital information. You can designate a place in your house to keep your address book. You can also use your computer. Remember to backup frequently.

"Things which matter most must never be at the mercy of things which matter least."

Johann Goethe

HABIT ~ 50

PLAN A PROJECT
BEFORE BEGINNING A PROJECT

The time you spend planning a task will repay itself many times over in implementation. Over planning, however, can waste time. A good rule is to reserve 10 to 20 percent of the time a project will take for planning. Planning provides a sense of direction and reduces challenges by anticipating potential obstacles.

"I see a person and know they
have what it takes to be
whatever they want to be—
if they choose to be!"

Jeffrey Lawrence Benjamin

HABIT ~ 51

NEVER GIVE UP
IN THE FACE OF FRUSTRATION

Tenacious people with good manners can never be stopped from accomplishing their goals and dreams. Look at each challenge or roadblock as a learning experience, an opportunity to practice, and a chance to develop your sense of humor. Create the habit of going until…

"Make voyages.
Attempt them.
There's nothing else."

Tennesse Williams

HABIT ~ 52

TAKE MINI-VACATIONS QUARTERLY

You don't have to take a week-long vacation to get rejuvenated. Take a Friday or Monday off and make it a three-day weekend. Go out of town with some friends to a nearby city or on a camping extravaganza. The idea is to go outside your usual living environment to experience something new. A quick vacation from work is not only a time to relax, it's a time to get a fresh perspective on life.

"The man who does not read good books has no advantage over the man who can't read them."

Mark Twain

HABIT ~ 53

EXERCISE MENTALLY

While your body responds favorably to physical exercise your mind will respond to consistent mental exercise. Opportunities present themselves daily and most people don't even recognize them because they are not prepared. If you are not in the habit, begin by reading five minutes a day— every day. Gradually increase this time period to one hour a day. Supplement your reading by listening to self-improvement and educational tapes while you drive.

"A successful person is the product of their life just the same as a failure. The difference is that successful people have learned how to use the same challenges we all face as opportunities to learn and grow."

Thomas J. Powell

HABIT ~ 54

CHOOSE TO LIVE YOUR LIFE

There truly is no good or bad, only our naming of an event makes it so. Never look at getting through a day, instead look at getting from a day. Life is simply a learning experience, so ask, "what can I learn from this and how can I use it to improve my life and the lives of others?" Your experiences are truly that—your experiences. They are what make you unique and special.

"Now is the time."

Martin Luther King, Jr.

HABIT ~ 55

PRACTICE PROPER POSTURE WHEN SITTING

Good posture communicates that you are alert and confident; it can also relieve many physical stresses. Poor posture is responsible for many health problems. Keep your feet flat on the floor. The height of your chair should allow your knees to form right angles. If the chair is too large, place a stool or books under your feet to raise your legs to this position. Relieve back stress by crossing your legs occasionally.

"From a man's face I can read character; if I can see him walk, I know his thoughts."

Petronius

HABIT ~ 56

PRACTICE GOOD POSTURE WHEN STANDING

Keep your head centered over your trunk. Habitually letting your head tilt forward may lead to chronic tension and pain in the neck muscles. Avoid slumping by keeping your shoulders down and back, and your chest up. But do not assume a stiff military posture; stay relaxed. Keep your pelvis straight. A forward tilt may place pressure on the lumbar disks. Keep your knees pointed forward and slightly flexed, not locked. If you must stand for prolonged periods, relieve back stress by propping one foot on a stool or rail.

"Hoping means seeing that the outcome you want is possible, and then working at it."

Bernie Siegel

HABIT ~ 57

PRACTICE DESK-BOUND STRETCHING

Amazingly, some of the most stressful jobs involve sitting at a desk. In one study, secretaries, managers and administrators were among those who suffered the highest rate of such stress-related illnesses. Simple stretching exercises serve to reduce stress by focusing your mind on something other than daily job pressures. Try this one: Keep both feet flat on the floor and drop your head toward your knees. Let your arms dangle freely. This relaxing pose will relieve tension in your lower back and increase circulation to your head.

"We cannot do
great things—only small
things with great love."

Mother Teresa

HABIT ~ 58

GET A PET

Tens of millions of Americans own pets. Now there is evidence that pets can reduce stress, as pet owners have known for a long time. Caring for a pet, researchers theorize, can provide a sense of belonging, opportunities for play and entertainment. Studies show that owning a pet, whether it's a dog, cat, bird or fish, can reduce the mild stress levels associated with minor, everyday frustrations. Animal ownership appears to be associated with improved health, lower blood pressure, reduced anxiety and at least a temporary reduction in stress levels.

"As soon as you trust yourself
you will know how to live."

Johann von Goethe

HABIT ~ 59

TAKE TIME OUT FOR YOURSELF

Time alone can be a prime place for renewal and peace. Make a conscious effort to take time out for yourself daily. Some find time early in the morning, some late at night. Find the time that works best for you.

"The world is but canvas to
our imaginations."

Henry David Thoreau

HABIT ~ 60

CREATE SOMETHING ARTISTIC

Creativity belongs to the artist in each of us. To create means to relate. When we paint, sculpt, write or dance, we fuse with imagination and get lost in our creative effort. The creative process absorbs us and we soon dissolve thoughts of anxiety and stress. This same ecstasy comes from an awesome athletic performance. Whatever your art form, it can be a masterful way to relieve stress.

"Great works are
performed not by strength,
but by perseverance."

Samuel Johnson

HABIT ~ 61

PRACTICE STRESS FREE EATING

Start your day with a balanced breakfast. Most people who skip breakfast or eat sugar and fatty foods in the morning, increase their propensity for a whole day of stressful imbalance. Choose plenty of low fat starches and fiber; carbohydrates tend to calm you down. Avoid eating large amounts of food later in the evening; it tends to disrupt sleep and cause more stress. The person who eats just what they need to feel comfortable and think clearly, greatly increases a relaxed productive lifestyle.

"Awareness is a key ingredient in success. If you have it, teach it. If you lack it, seek it."

Michael B. Kitson

HABIT ~ 62

LOOK FOR SOLUTIONS, NOT BLAME

When confronted with a challenge, especially a recurring one, it is important to take the time and effort to look for solutions. If the challenge proves to be unsolvable in the present moment remember that there are no accidents, only learning experiences.

"If a man will devote his time to securing facts in an impartial, objective way, his worries will usually evaporate in light of knowledge."

Herbert E. Hawkes

HABIT ~ 63

GET THE FACTS

Most people make decisions emotionally rather than intellectually and then work toward supporting their decisions with facts. Intuition generally won't lie, but emotions often do. Help your intuition by getting as many impartial facts as you can and writing them down as you collect them. When the time comes to make the decision you can simply weigh the facts without stress.

"The ideal man takes joy in doing favors for others."

Aristotle

HABIT ~ 64

DO NOT EXPECT GRATITUDE

It is normal for people to forget to be grateful. Normal does not excuse it; nonetheless, we must learn not to be disappointed by others' lack of manners and instead rejoice when we do occasionally receive a thank you. When you give simply for the joy of giving without expectation of gratitude from the receiver, your spirit grows immensely.

"Truth is immortal;
error is mortal."

Mary Baker Eddy

HABIT ~ 65

MAKE LEMONADE

Life is composed of a series of experiences. What we choose to take from each experience determines the quality and success of our life. Anytime you feel limited or unhappy by an experience, take time to examine the event to see how *you* could have changed it, avoided it, or overcome the part that made the experience less than ideal. The next time you are presented with a similar challenge you will have already planned to succeed.

"Rest is not a matter
of doing absolutely nothing.
Rest is repair."

Daniel W. Josselyn

HABIT ~ 66

RECREATE THROUGH RECREATION

The average human heart is beating only nine of twenty-four hours a day. For each beat there is a rest. Design each day, week, month and year with time to rest. Protect this time as though your life depended on it—because it does.

"All things are yours."

I Corinthians 3:21

HABIT ~ 67

AFFIRM WHAT YOU WANT

We live in a world of abundance. Affirm to yourself anytime you are feeling a moment of lack: *An Infinite law obeys me. An Infinite mind guides me. An Infinite peace sustains me. An Infinite abundance supplies me. An Infinite love enfolds me. An Infinite health renews me. An Infinite presence transforms me. An Infinite God loves me.*

"Begin to weave and
God will give the thread."

German Proverb

HABIT ~ 68

LAUGH OFTEN

Keep a book of jokes in your personal library, a video of your favorite slapstick comedy and an audiotape of your favorite comedian. Use these as tools to make you laugh when you feel your stress level rising. Laughter cleanses the system and needs to be part of your daily regime.

"Mental health is an ongoing
process of dedication to
reality at all costs."

M. Scott Peck, M.D.

HABIT ~ 69

EXAMINE THE EVENTS OF YOUR DAY

A complete dedication to the truth requires a continuous and never-ending stringent self-examination of your life. To minimize stress it is very important to be truthful with yourself. Keep a journal and at the end of each day ask if your present thoughts and actions are moving you closer to or farther from the person you want to be.

"A mediocre idea that generates enthusiasm will go further than a great idea that inspires no one."

Mary Kay Ash

HABIT ~ 70

READ THE BOOKS THAT CHILDREN READ

To improve communication with children meet them in the books they are reading. Reading together is important, but the real value comes in understanding how your child's mind is expanding each day. Children's books bridge the generation gap as they remind us where we came from and which direction our children are heading.

"Get what you can and
keep what you have;
that's the way to get rich."

Scottish Proverb

HABIT ~ 71

LEARN TO APOLOGIZE

When you realize you've made a mistake, take immediate steps to correct it and make an apology to anyone who was hurt or inconvenienced. The habit of being proactive requires you to take personal responsibility for your attitude and actions. A sincere "I am sorry," accompanied by action to correct and prevent the mistake, goes a long way.

"I have learned that success is to be measured not so much by the position that one has reached in life as by the obstacles which he has overcome while trying to succeed."

Booker T. Washington

144

HABIT ~ 72

REJOICE IN YOUR SUCCESSES

Keep a simple chart of successes for each week and update it daily. At the end of the week review the chart to see how many successes you achieved. When you are feeling challenged look back through these charts and remember how successful you truly are and have been.

"When I can no longer create anything, I'll be done for."

Coco Chanel

HABIT ~ 73

LOOK AT YOUR HARVEST

Look at the current harvest in your life (your level of happiness, health, wealth, connection to God and others, etc.), and then look at the sower—you—and take credit where it is due. Don't forget to also take responsibility for areas that need improvement. If you are dissatisfied with any part of your life, be thankful that it is through *your* thoughts, actions and habits that you can make changes.

"The secret of success of every man who has ever been successful lies in the fact that he formed the habit of doing those things failures don't like to do."

A. Jackson King

HABIT ~ 74

REPLACE LIMITING HABITS WITH EMPOWERING ONES

Studies show that 21 days of consistent behavior forms a habit. Take an inventory of your habits and where they are taking you. Gradually replace your limiting habits with empowering ones. For example, try watching half an hour less television a day and replace that time with power-walking, playing with your children or reading.

149

"A prudent person profits from personal experience, a wise one from the experience of others."

Joseph Collins

HABIT ~ 75

STUDY OTHER PEOPLE'S EXPERIENCES

The Bible is complete with both stories of people who succeeded and people who failed. It is important to study each side. If you want to be calm and relaxed, find a calm and relaxed person and study their actions and words while they are in a stressful situation; but also find a "stressed out" person and do the same study. Compare and contrast them and you will understand why and how the calm and relaxed person's strategies work.

"There is only one person in control of your life—and that person is you!"

Jeffrey Lawrence Benjamin

HABIT ~ 76

CREATE A POSITIVE ATMOSPHERE

The atmosphere of attitudes and behaviors surrounding you is nearly as important as the atmosphere surrounding the earth. A positive atmosphere allows you to laugh and learn from mistakes. The best part of being positive is that negative people generally can't stand being around you for too long—making room for other positive people to get closer to you.

"No one is jealous of a loser."

Tom Hopkins

HABIT ~ 77

SURROUND YOURSELF
WITH SUCCESSFUL PEOPLE

If your friends, family, lover, coworkers and boss are not supportive during the peaks and valleys of your life it is imperative that you surround yourself with positive influences. In each of your current and new relationships ask the other person: "Over the next three years how do you see our relationship developing and what benefits do you feel you are receiving from being associated with me?" Share your answers to the same question with them.

"Successful people do what successful people do, and failures do what failures do; and if the failures did what the successful do, the failures would be successful."

Thomas J. Powell

HABIT ~ 78

VISIT YOUR FAVORITE SPA

Be good to yourself. Find a spa that relaxes your mind and body and energizes your soul. Enjoy a facial, reflexology or a full body massage. Treat yourself often.

"People with goals succeed because they know where they're going."

Earl Nightingale

HABIT ~ 79

BE EXCITED BY CHANGE

When confronted with a new situation say: "I can't wait to see what good comes of this." When you look for the good, just as when you look for the bad, you usually can find some. Choose to look for the good by knowing the simple truth that life only happens because of change.

"Through imagination, we can visualize the uncreated worlds of potential that lie within us."

Stephen R. Covey

HABIT ~ 80

USE VISUALIZATION TO GET GROUNDED

Visualization is the process of creating a picture in your mind's eye of an imaginary experience. When things seem like they are in chaos and you don't feel grounded, take a broad stance. Close your eyes. Breathe deeply in through your nose and out through your mouth. Continue to do this while you imagine that you are a tree, rooted in the place that you stand.

"There is no security
on this earth;
there is only opportunity."

Douglas MacArthur

HABIT ~ 81

ESTABLISH A SAVINGS ACCOUNT

You can deposit money in your savings account manually, however it's easier and more convenient using automation. Each month have a certain amount deducted from your checking account and deposited in a savings account. The nice thing is that you forget about it and your money grows with each month. You can use this money for a nest egg or for emergency purposes. Saving generates a certain sense of peace of mind knowing that you have more alternatives and choices available.

"When anyone tells me I can't
do anything. I'm just not
listening any more."

Florence Griffith Joyner

HABIT ~ 82

LEAVE THE TELEVISION OFF FOR A WEEK

The decision to make this drastic change alone (for most people) will release creative energy. Take the challenge and leave it off! Create your own life—the one you've imagined.

"The important thing is this:
to be able at any moment to
sacrifice what we are for what
we can become."

Charles Du Bos

HABIT ~ 83

COUNT TO 10 WHEN
A CHALLENGING SITUATION ARISES

Allow yourself the relief of a defused situation by giving yourself a timeout. Step away and take deep breaths as you count to 10. The moment will take on a different meaning.

"Be glad of life because it gives you the chance to love and to work and to look at the stars."

Henry van Dyke

HABIT ~ 84

GO STAR GAZING

Assume your favorite star gazing position. Let your mind create or just drift in the wonderment above. Fall asleep as you completely relax under a sea of stars.

"I believe the ultimate path to enlightenment is the cultivation of gratitude."

Anthony Robbins

HABIT ~ 85

CREATE A GRATITUDE LIST

Scribe 100 blessings in your life. The list is endless, and the relaxing benefits will affect you as soon as you begin. Pin this list on the wall and keep adding to it.

"Never put off till tomorrow
what you can do today."

Thomas Jefferson

HABIT ~ 86

KEEP YOUR IMMEDIATE ENVIRONMENT ORGANIZED

This is one of the easiest and most effective stress relievers. You may not be aware of the incredible stress a cluttered work environment can have on you. Wasting time looking for something, or even having a mess in your peripheral vision raises your tension. Take the time to get and stay organized. You will love the empowering and relaxed feeling you will have from a continually organized environment.

"Live all you can;
it's a mistake not to."

Henry Adams

HABIT ~ 87

MAKE LOVE

Make love with your significant other. Truly relax and let out all your emotions with no inhibitions. Ask your partner to do the same and feel your body relax and the stress and tension fade away.

"I'm not a teacher,
but an awakener."

Robert Frost

HABIT ~ 88

CRY IF YOU FEEL LIKE IT

People can save themselves loads of stress by allowing the tears to flow. It doesn't take an expert to measure the calming effects that crying can have on us in helping ease a highly emotional and stressful state of mind. Go ahead, let all it out. Don't carry it with you. You will be better off, especially in the long run.

"Whatever you steadfastly direct your attention to, will come into your life and dominate it."

Emmet Fox

HABIT ~ 89

DON'T READ OR WATCH THE NEWS FOR AN EXTENDED PERIOD OF TIME

You will be informed of all the news (bad news) that may be "important" in our society without watching television. The news will come in from friends, co-workers and numerous other sources whether you like it or not. Stop watching the news and spend that valuable time enjoying life.

"Adopt the secret of nature;
her secret is patience."

Ralph Waldo Emerson

HABIT ~ 90

WATCH YOUR FAVORITE MOVIE

Make a list of your 10 favorite movies of all time. You can purchase, record or rent each. When you feel anxious or on the proverbial edge, pop one in and "lose yourself" for a couple of hours.

"I must govern the clock, not
be governed by it."

Golda Meir

HABIT ~ 91

SCHEDULE THE NEXT DAY'S BUSINESS BEFORE YOU GO TO SLEEP EACH NIGHT

This strategy alone will relieve most anxieties and tensions you otherwise allow to fester. Let your subconscious loose on tomorrow's opportunities while you sleep peacefully. Make your list; prioritize and relax.

"The beautiful souls are they
that are universal, open and
ready for all things."

Michel Montaigne

HABIT ~ 92

BE VULNERABLE

Let your guard down. Experience life and all its emotions with the willingness to truly let everyone and everything see and feel you as you really are. Enjoy the freedom this brings.

"Failure is impossible."

Susan B. Anthony

HABIT ~ 93

DO ONE "THING" YOU'VE BEEN PUTTING OFF

Make a list and prioritize it. Schedule one "thing" per week that you've been putting off. The satisfaction will fulfill you and help you to feel at peace with your inner self.

"I personally measure success in terms of the contributions an individual makes to her or his fellow human beings."

Margaret Mead

HABIT ~ 94

CALL AN OLD FRIEND

There are no friends like the friends you've known the longest. They have the innate ability to help you see your life and challenges in a positive perspective. Old friends help to bring out the kid in you. They let you talk your way out of stressful or potentially stressful situations and renew your hope and positive attitude.

"I always prefer to believe the
best of everybody—it
saves so much trouble."

Rudyard Kipling

HABIT ~ 95

FIND THE BEST IN EVERYONE

If you are serious about reducing your stress, this habit will have an amazing effect on your life. You will reduce your stress level immeasurably and instantly, and you will want to become an expert in this area because of the way it makes YOU feel. Everyone benefits. Ask, probe, find the best in everyone and enjoy the incredible rewards that come with it.

"The man who moved
a mountain was the
one who began carrying
away small stones."

Chinese Proverb

HABIT ~ 96

TAKE VITAMIN
AND MINERAL SUPPLEMENTS

A fully functioning human being is someone who finds balance in his life. Taking supplements not only helps you balance physically, but mentally as well. Knowing that you are helping your physical body relieves stressful thoughts and worries about sickness and disease. Supplement what you know you are not getting in your diet—and relax.

"There is a great deal of
unmapped country within us."

George Eliot

HABIT ~ 97

ENJOY NATURE HIKING

When it comes to stress it is always a good idea to "get back to nature" and go outdoors to "smell the roses." A nature hike of any length usually does the trick. Take your time and stop often to just observe your surroundings. Feel the tension leave your mind, body and soul. Carefully plan your hike to fit your level of enjoyment.

"Have to and get to—both are choices. One is negative and one is positive. Choose the right one and it can change your life."

Michael B. Kitson

HABIT ~ 98

RELAX IN A HOT TUB OR JACUZZI

You can use peaceful music to enhance this experience. Perhaps some sounds of the ocean or a rainstorm. Find a position where you can completely relax. Listen to the sounds, feel the warmth of the water, become aware of your muscles relaxing as the jets gently massage you. Let your mind wander into a peaceful state.

"The minute you think
you don't need to improve
is the minute you
have a huge problem."

Jeffrey Lawrence Benjamin

HABIT ~ 99

ATTEND STRESS MANAGEMENT WORKSHOPS

Whether you read it or hear it in any fashion it is best to keep your mind on living in peace, relaxation and harmony. Attend a workshop and keep all your notes and the materials handy. Read as little as one paragraph per day and you will see and feel a marked difference in your life and demeanor. Challenge yourself to practice one relaxation technique per day from this book.

"Conviction is worthless
unless it is converted
into conduct."

Thomas Carlyle

HABIT ~ 100

UNPLUG OR TURN OFF YOUR PHONES

An important task is always easier with no distractions, especially those of phones. Schedule a time to return messages. If you carry a phone with you wherever you go, turn it off when you are not using it. If you must make a call while driving, pull over to dial, then use a head set on one ear only. You may be saving more than stress.

"Look and you will
find it—what is unsought
will go undetected."

Sophocles

HABIT ~ 101

DECIDE YOUR DESTINY OR IT WILL BE DECIDED FOR YOU

If you have not decided who, where and what you want to be, it is being decided for you by someone else. Write, as fast as you can, without much thought, 101 goals you would like to achieve before you die. Pretend you are a kid again and that Santa will bring you anything you want but you must write it down to get it. After you complete the list take time to prioritize it and establish deadlines for each goal.

Write your own habits for breaking through stress…

J. T. and Lindé Ravizé have used their superlative photography and poetry to encourage legislators and the public towards exceptional stewardship of the natural environment. Their award winning work is being used extensively to support efforts to preserve Lake Tahoe, Big Sur, Wine Country, and other imperiled natural places.

Using their "Hearts of Light" book series, and museum shows around the country, they have reached a broad and enthusiastic audience and have become influential voices for the natural world.

Visit their website: www.aframeofmind.com
E-mail: jtr@aframeofmind.com
Or call their gallery "A Frame of Mind Gallery" 775-588-8081

Jeffrey Benjamin

For more than 15 years author and speaker Jeffrey Benjamin has dedicated his life to passionately sharing career and personal achievement strategies with both small and large companies. He published his first book at the age of 23 and is the co-author of the acclaimed book series *Real Life Habits for Success.* He is also the host of his own television and radio show featuring leaders with real life success stories. Jeffrey is the founder of BREAKTHROUGH TRAINING, and a performance coach energizing thousands of people every month.

www.breakthroughtraining.com
toll free: 800.547.9868

Training & Coaching
Keynotes & Retreats

Mike Kitson

Mike is the founder and president of On-Call Graphics, Inc., a full-service creative studio in Reno, Nevada. OCG's mission is to work as a team, attract clients we enjoy, deliver uncompromising quality in a relaxing and creative environment. Mike holds his B.A. in Journalism from the University of Nevada. He has published over 20 books.

He is also the founder of the Forward Thinking Group, a group of consultants and coaches offering "Therapy for Business."

www.oncallgraphics.com
toll free: 800.825.0448

John Oliver

John Oliver's work has taken him around the world and his diverse educational background includes degrees in Criminal Justice, English Literature and Kinesiology. John shares this knowledge and his experiences in life and business with individuals and fortune 500 companies.

John is a successful entrepreneur and is the keynote speaker, writer, and LifeCoach that helps you experience the joy of everyday life.

JohnOliver.com

Thomas J. Powell

Tom Powell is passionate about putting people into homes and helping them realize the American dream of homeownership. He is the President of *Into*homes Mortgage Services LLC, one of the leading mortgage lenders in Nevada. He speaks regularly to business, educational and community groups on success, motivation and leadership. He attributes his own success to constant investment in personal and professional development, both for himself and his employees. He shares a home with his wife and four children.

 toll free: 877-*into*homes *into*homes.com

Order Form

Please send me Break Through Your Stress for $8.95 per book plus shipping:

Quantity: $8.95 per book .... _____

Shipping: $2.00 per book .... _____

Total cost of book(s) and shipping cost: .... _____

For large quantity orders (10) books or more, please call 800.825.0448 for special discount pricing.

Full Name: _____

Mailing Address: _____

City: _____ State: _____ Zip: _____

MC/VISA/AMEX# _____ Exp._____

Check / Money Order for $_____ Payable to: World Vision Publishing, LLC

Daytime telephone number: (   ) _____

Signature: _____

Mail to: World Vision Publishing, P.O. Box 7332, Reno, Nevada, 89510.
Or call: 800.825.0448 to place your order today!

216